D1432903

Memories

Celebrating Our Family

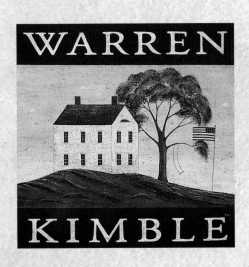

WARREN KIMBLE
American Folk Artist

APPLE TREE

Memories

Celebrating Our Family

Preserving special moments of everyday living can be a labor of love and a work of art.

In this special *Memories* book, best-known living folk artist Warren Kimble

contributes some of his best paintings with specially designed pages for you

to place your photographs and favorite family keepsakes.

For a starting point in recording your family memories, begin with yourself,

include your special "someone," and branch out to each of your extended families.

Then you're ready to collect thoughts, photographs, and keepsakes of those with whom

you are creating everyday memories—your children, friends and family, and even your pets!

Warren Kimble's *Memories* is conveniently-sized to accommodate a standard

4 x 6-inch photograph and printed on acid-free paper to protect your photographs for the future.

You'll want to use acid-free tape for securing your photographs and an acid-free pen for recording

your special memories. Short phrases are provided to help get your thoughts flowing and

then you're off and running. In no time at all, you'll have a wonderful book filled with your

own unique memories to share with friends, family, and future generations. Enjoy!

LIFETIME MATES

Beginnings

_____

_____

_____

_____

_____

_____

_____

_____

_____

_____

Place photo here

Place photo here

Our Keepsakes

NOAH'S ARK

Our Family

_____

_____

_____

_____

_____

_____

_____

_____

_____

_____

Place photo here

Place photo here

Place photo here

Place photo here

Place photo here

SAILOR BEAR

Our Children

_____

_____

_____

_____

_____

_____

_____

_____

_____

_____

Place photo here

Place photo here

Place photo here

WARREN KIMBLE

SPRING PANEL

Springtime Memories

Place photo here

SUMMER PANEL

Summer Fun

_____

_____

_____

_____

_____

_____

_____

_____

_____

_____

_____

Place photo here

FALL PANEL

Fall Celebrations

_____

_____

_____

_____

_____

_____

_____

_____

_____

_____

_____

Place photo here

© WARREN KIMBLE

WINTER PANEL

Winter Wonderland

_____

_____

_____

_____

_____

_____

_____

_____

_____

_____

_____

Place photo here

COASTAL BREEZE II

Our Family Vacation

_____

_____

_____

_____

_____

_____

_____

_____

_____

_____

_____

Place photo here

HOUSE WITH QUILT

Home Sweet Home

_____

_____

_____

_____

_____

_____

_____

_____

_____

Place photo here

SUMMER DELIGHT

Eating Together

_____

_____

_____

_____

_____

_____

_____

_____

_____

_____

Place photo here

Family Meal Traditions

_____   _____

_____   _____

_____   _____

_____   _____

_____   _____

Cooks We Remember

_____   _____

_____   _____

_____   _____

Favorite Family Recipes

_____   _____

_____   _____

_____   _____

_____   _____

_____   _____

_____   _____

_____   _____

_____   _____

_____   _____

_____   _____

ROUND BARN

A Special Place We Like To Go

_____

_____

_____

_____

_____

_____

_____

_____

_____

_____

Place photo here

LAKE TROUT

Our Favorite Hobbies

_____

_____

_____

_____

_____

_____

_____

_____

_____

_____

_____

Place photo here

BIRDIE

FLY BALL

Favorite Sports

_____

_____

_____

_____

_____

_____

_____

_____

_____

Place photo here

THREE CHEERS FOR THE RED WHITE AND BLUE

©WARREN KIMBLE

THREE CHEERS

God Bless America!

_____

_____

_____

_____

_____

_____

_____

_____

_____

_____

Place photo here

WARREN KIMBLE, 1989

CLIFF

Our Favorite Pets

_____

_____

_____

_____

_____

_____

_____

_____

_____

_____

Place photo here

SCHOOLHOUSE

Schooldays

_____

_____

_____

_____

_____

_____

_____

_____

_____

_____

Place photo here

Place photo here

Place photo here

Schooldays Keepsakes

Schooldays Keepsakes

PLAID CATS

Special Times Together

_____

_____

_____

_____

_____

_____

_____

_____

_____

_____

_____

Place photo here

Place photo here

Place photo here

ROLLING HILLS

Places We've Visited

_____

_____

_____

_____

_____

_____

_____

_____

_____

Place photo here

Places We've Visited

Places We've Visited

Kissing Cows

People We Love

_____

_____

_____

_____

_____

_____

_____

_____

_____

Place photo here

Place photo here

NATURE'S BOUNTY

Things We Are Thankful For

_____ _____

_____ _____

_____ _____

_____ _____

_____ _____

_____ _____

_____ _____

_____ _____

Warren Kimble

"*I hope your memories are as wonderful as mine.*"

ABOUT THE ARTIST

The world of Warren Kimble is delightfully simple and welcoming.
In a restored nineteenth-century barn that serves as his studio,
Warren offers visitors the chance to see arts, antiques,
and rare items that reflect a lifetime of painting and collecting.
Now regarded as America's best-known living folk artist,
Warren Kimble continues to work as he has done for the past
forty years. By painting every day and maintaining an active role
in his community, Warren has demonstrated what one critic has
said are priorities in the right order: "Good folks and good folk art."